REFLECTIONS OF A QUIET STORM

A Grief Memoir

By

Farra Collins

Published by Angel of Mine Publishing

DEDICATION

To my mother, whose love still lingers in every part of me...

In loving memory of my mother

"The Lord is close to the brokenhearted and saves those who are crushed in spirit."

— Psalm 34:18

ACKNOWLEDGMENTS

To every person who has walked alongside me in grief, Thank You. To those who listened when I had no words, cried with me when I broke down, and stood in the gap when I couldn't stand for myself, you are part of this story.

Thank you to my Aunt Margie, for being a light in my life when things felt dark. Your love and presence shaped the woman I became.

To my father and brother: we survived. And we did so together. I love you more than words could ever capture.

The greatest thanks of all to my mother. Thank you for loving me first.

ABOUT THE AUTHOR

Farra Collins is a storyteller, encourager, and woman of deep faith. Born and raised in Mississippi, Farra began journaling as a young girl, turning her personal pain into words that now serve to uplift others. Her heart for family, faith, and healing shines through everything she writes.

Reflections of a Quiet Storm is her first published work—a deeply personal memoir honoring her late mother and the journey through grief that shaped her into the woman she is today.

When she's not writing, Farra can be found homeschooling, working from home, laughing with her family, or dreaming up her next adventure. Follow her journey and future works at Angel of Mine Publishing.

Contents

CHAPTER 1

THE DAY THE STORM CAME

The day my mom died was the day after Valentine's Day. A day I will never forget. The Sunday before, my dad sat me and my brother down and told us that our mom was in a coma. He gave us time to cry and process before we went to the hospital to see her one last time.

I can still remember that Sunday the smell of the hospital still lingers in my memory. The room was cold, machines beeped, and wires ran everywhere. My Aunt Bee sat in the corner singing hymns. I felt like I was suffocating, the grief was so strong. My aunt, the one we had been staying with, was in the room too, and I was confused because she wasn't supposed to be there, she had planned to travel out of town that day for work.

Then my cousin walked in with tears in his eyes, and I couldn't hold it in anymore. I dismissed myself. My aunt and brother followed to check on me. I just told them I needed to catch my breath.

That night, my brother broke down and cried for our mom, not the person we had seen in that hospital bed. He sobbed. That night, and for the rest of that week, I held him every night as he cried himself to sleep.

Friday came. We went to school like normal. After school, we usually got off at our grandmother's house with our cousins, but that day no adults were home. We waited outside with our older cousin Keneshia, sitting in the yard watching cars pass by. My cousin Keneshia, always the jokester, kept us laughing.

Then I saw my grandparents' car pull up, and right behind them, my dad. My heart sank. They never left my mom alone at the hospital. My dad got out of the car and walked toward me.

I felt numb.

He leaned in, and he told me the news.

My legs felt like jelly. My dad caught me before I could fall to the ground.

CHAPTER 2

TOO YOUNG TO UNDERSTAND, OLD ENOUGH TO HURT

The day of my mother's funeral felt like a blur like I was floating outside of my own body. I remember it, but I do not feel it. Not in the way that I felt the day after.

That Sunday, the day after we buried her, was the day everything hit me.

By then, the house was quiet again. The visitors had left, the casseroles had been eaten, and the doorbell had stopped ringing. We were left alone with our new normal. That morning, my dad said, "Let's go get some breakfast." So, we did. Just me, my dad, and my little brother, sitting at a table at Burger King.

We had just gotten our food. We were talking casually, trying to make sense of the last two weeks. I was mid-chew when the weight of it all slammed into me like a freight train. One moment I was eating, and the next, I was bawling. My dad was still talking, but I couldn't hold back anymore.

That was the moment I realized it was final.

The casket had been closed.

The grave had been filled.

My mother was not coming home.

As long as her body was at the funeral home, a part of me still held onto some tiny hope. But that hope was buried with her. And in the middle of that Burger King, I broke. I cried. And I did not care who saw.

When we got home, I went straight to my room. I did not want to talk. I did not want to be strong. I just wanted to cry and I did. I laid down in my bed and cried until I fell asleep, physically, and emotionally exhausted.

That day, I stayed in my room. I needed the silence.

There were still reminders everywhere. My mom had received so many flowers; they covered the entire floor of our garage. After the repass, people delivered dozens more. My dad even took pictures of the sea of bouquets. She had taught so many students over the years the outpouring of love from them and the community was overwhelming but comforting. The chapel at her funeral was packed wall to wall with flowers.

That Sunday marked the beginning of my reality. And even though my dad had offered for all of us to sleep in his bed for comfort, I eventually told him I needed to go back to my room. I was the only girl, and as comforting as it was, I needed space to process.

What broke me emotionally on Sunday tried to break me all over again on Monday.

Because life didn't stop.

Monday came and with it, school. I had choir competition that day. I had only missed one day of school the week my mom died. She passed on a Friday, and I was back in school on Monday. I went every day that week except for the following Friday when we visited her body. There was never a pause, never a moment to really process the weight of what had happened.

Grief didn't get an invitation to school.

That Monday during the bus ride to the choir competition, a friend told me she had seen me at the funeral but said, "You didn't really cry." I looked at her and said, "I was in a daze. Yesterday was the day I really broke down."

No one really asked me how I was doing. Not like they meant it. Except Marcus. He and Tamara came to the funeral and Marcus told me something I have never forgotten. He said, "Take care of yourself. Make sure you take time for you." That moment stayed with me. It was the first time someone acknowledged that I was a person—not just a child, not just someone expected to stay strong.

Everyone else seemed to only repeat the same thing: You have to be strong. You have to keep going. You have to make your mom proud.

And I did. That became my mission: to make my mom proud of everything I did. I became consistent. I worked harder. I put my all into everything because I felt like my grief had to serve a purpose. I did not give myself space to fall apart.

But the one person who consistently showed up for me emotionally was my Aunt Margie. From age 13 to age 25 until the day she passed she was my rock. You will read more about her later in this book, but her presence in my life was a lifeline I didn't even know I needed.

There is one last memory I want to hold onto from that time. When we pulled up to the funeral home for my mom's service, my anxiety was high. My nerves were shot. But when I stepped inside, I saw my little niece Erica just two years old at the time standing in the foyer. In that moment, it felt like God had sent me a reminder that I would be okay. I bent down, hugged her, and held her hand. We walked together for a moment, and even though I had to join the line, I carried that calm with me.

Erica was my reminder that light still existed.

That I could keep going.

That just maybe I would survive the storm.

CHAPTER 3

THE WEIGHT OF BEING OKAY

When my mom passed, I made an unspoken decision—I was going to be okay so everyone else could be okay. I started trying to be everything to everybody. I checked in on how others were feeling. I made sure people smiled. I smiled too, even when I did not feel like it. That became my way of coping.

But looking back, I was not healing I was hiding. I was not grieving, I was people-pleasing. And in trying to make sure everyone else had peace, I started silencing my own pain.

That summer after my mom died, life seemed like it was returning to normal, at least on the outside. My brother and I spent our days at home with my cousin Keneshia during the day, and for a moment, we settled into a new routine.

Keneshia's church had just started a dance ministry. We spent hours practicing routines and dancing around the house, letting the music drown out the silence that grief had left behind. We played my Mary Mary CD on repeat. Her favorite song was "Can't Give Up Now." That song hits differently now. At the time, it felt like a beat we could move to but now, it feels like a message we were surviving by. We were kids, but we were in a storm. And somehow, the music helped us dance through it.

One of the constants that summer was my grandmother. She has always been my rock. When everything around me felt uncertain, Granny was steady. During those long, hot Mississippi summers, she would go on her regular store runs, and she never failed to call and ask if I wanted to ride with her. I always said yes. It was not just about getting out of the house it was about being with her. Granny was my road dog, and riding shotgun with her became a small pocket of peace in the middle of my storm.

Even in my mom's final days, Granny showed up for us in every way she could. She helped me make grocery runs for our house, helped keep the pieces of our day-to-day life together when everything else was falling apart. I do not think I realized it at the time, but my mom had molded me to be independent and a caregiver from an early age. She raised me to be capable, to carry responsibility, and to help where help was needed. So, when I started stepping into those roles and making lists, helping my dad, keeping things organized it felt natural. Like I was doing what I was supposed to do.

But deep down, I was not just being helpful

I was trying to keep things from falling apart

I was trying to hold us together

Because if I stayed busy, I wouldn't have time to fall apart myself.

Looking back, I didn't realize how much those early responsibilities were shaping who I would become. At thirteen, I was not just a grieving daughter—I was already becoming a woman who would struggle to rest, to ask for help, to say, "I'm not okay." I learned how to push through. I learned how to keep going, even when I was breaking inside. I thought that is what strong women did.

I did not know I was building a wall. Brick by brick, every time I swallowed a tear, every time I put someone else's needs before my own, every time I chose silence over asking for support, I was reinforcing the idea that my feelings didn't matter as much. That being useful, being dependable, being "okay" was the way to earn love, to feel safe.

The truth is, I was praised for being mature.

People told me I was so strong, so responsible, so helpful.

And I was.

But no one stopped to ask, "Are you tired?"

"Are you scared?"

"Do you need a break?"

So I became the girl who never needed anything.

And that girl? She grew into a woman who had to unlearn the idea that love is something you earn by doing.

It would take years for me to realize that just being just existing was enough.

That I didn't have to hold the world together to be worthy of rest, of support, of softness.

That little girl in the storm… she was doing the best she could.

And I'm so proud of her.

But what I didn't know then was that grief wasn't done shaping me it was just beginning.

Reflection Prompt

Think about a milestone you experienced without someone you loved.

- What did that moment teach you about strength or vulnerability?
- How do you carry your loved one's memory with you into new experiences?
- What new traditions or acts of love have you created in their honor?

Farra Collins

Quote for Reflection

> *There is no expiration date on the*
> *love between a mother and her child.*

— Unknown

Scripture

She is clothed with strength and dignity; she can laugh at the days to come.

— Proverbs 31:25

CHAPTER 4

A SECOND MOTHER

There are some people who step in when the world falls apart—who do not try to replace what was lost but instead become a light in the aftermath. For me, that person was my Aunt Margie.

Tee Margie was not just my aunt. She was my second mom on earth. My breath of fresh air when the weight of grief became too much to carry.

After my mother passed away, she became my safe place. Saturday nights were our time. We would spend them together, and in those small, simple routines, she gave me something to look forward to again. She never tried to fill my mother's shoes—but somehow, she managed to help me walk without falling apart. Her love was steady, gentle, and deeply rooted. Being around her felt like being seen and held at the same time.

Years later, when I became pregnant with my daughter, I found myself longing for my mother more than ever. That was one of the hardest years of my life. Becoming a mother without your own mother by your side is a kind of ache that words can barely touch. On the anniversary of my mom's passing, I remember sitting on the bathroom floor, pregnant and overwhelmed, and whispering to her, 'I'm not okay.'

It felt like grief was circling back to meet me in a new form—one that was tangled up in joy and fear and the longing for her guidance. I did not know how to do this without her.

But once again, Tee Margie showed up.

She had never been one to drive on the highway, but when I called her on my way to the hospital, she did not hesitate. She offered to be by my side. She was there for me in the ways I needed most quietly, consistently, and lovingly.

And then… grief came for me again.

Just four months after giving birth to my daughter, only two hours after picking her up from my aunt's house I got the call that shattered me.

My aunt was gone. Killed in a car accident.

It did not feel real. It could not be real.

This grief stung in a way that knocked the wind out of me. It was unexpected, brutal, and confusing. I wanted answers from God. Why? You already took my mom. And now you are taking the closest thing I had to her? Why is this happening to me—again?

The loss of my Aunt Margie felt like losing my mother all over again. Only this time, I was not thirteen. I was a mother myself, still trying to find my footing. Her death was a thief in the night, stealing peace, safety, and the last sense of maternal comfort I had left.

Reflection Prompt

- Who has shown up for you during your hardest moments?
- What lessons did they leave behind that still guide you today?
- How do you carry their love with you, even after they are gone?

Take a few moments to write down how someone has supported you through grief. What small things did they do that made a significant difference?

Quote

*"Some souls come into our lives and leave
footprints on our hearts. When they
leave, we are never the same—not
because they're gone, but because their
love stays with us forever."*

Scripture

"As a mother comforts her child, so will I comfort you."

—Isaiah 66:13

CHAPTER 5

MOTHERLESS MILESTONES

Milestones are hard.

They still are.

Every time I reach one—every degree earned, every birthday celebrated, every accomplishment marked—grief rushes in like a wave I thought I had already swum through. It does not matter how many years pass. The absence does not soften with time, it just hides in the quiet moments, waiting.

I have now had twenty-three birthdays without her.

And somehow, each one still feels like something is missing.

People say, "Happy Birthday," and I smile. I celebrated. I am grateful. But deep down, there is always a part of me that aches. A part that still whispers, I wish she could be here... just one more time.

Christmas is hard.

It is supposed to be a season of joy, family, warmth. But for me, it is also a countdown. Because after Christmas in 2001, my mom went into the hospital—and she never came home.

The holidays do not just mark the end of the year for me.

They mark the beginning of the end.

Valentine's Day?

It has never been the same. People talk about love and roses and chocolate—but for me, Valentine's Day is the last day I ever had a mother. Because the next day, February 15th, is when my life changed forever. The day the world stopped spinning the way it used to.

But now… I am a mother too.

And that changes everything.

I have a daughter.

She is growing up in a world where her grandmother lives in stories, pictures, and the sound of her name in our prayers.

And because of that, because of what I lost I am intentional about what I give her.

On the holidays that used to break me, I now choose to build memories.

On Valentine's Day, we exchange little gifts. I tell her how deeply she is loved, and we celebrate love in all its forms.

On Christmas, we decorate together, bake cookies, and make joy tangible. Because I want her to feel the magic not the mourning.

And on my birthday, I let her see me smile.

Not because the ache is gone… but because I have learned how to carry it and still live.

When I earned my master's degree, I remember feeling so overwhelmed with pride and grief.

My push to finish came from knowing that my mom completed her master's degree while going through brain cancer. She was sick, but she still pushed through. That was the kind of strength she modeled for me.

So, when I felt tired or discouraged, I thought of her.

She did not get to walk the stage—but neither did I.

15

I graduated during the COVID pandemic, and though I earned my degree, I never got to have that moment, that celebration.

Still, in my heart, I walked across that stage with her.

Every time I push myself further, I carry her legacy with me.

That is what keeps me going.

In creating new traditions for my daughter, I have slowly begun to heal the wounds left in me.

They have not disappeared—but somehow, they do not sting as sharply when I see her laugh when I hear her say, "I love you, Mommy."

She does not know it yet, but she is helping me reimagine every milestone.

Not as something I must survive.

But, something I get to share.

Quote

> *"Grief never ends... but it changes.*
> *It is a passage, not a place to stay.*
> *Grief is not a sign of weakness, nor*
> *a lack of faith, it is the price of*
> *love."*

Scripture

> *"The Lord is close to the brokenhearted and saves those who are crushed in spirit."*

> **—Psalm 34:18**

CHAPTER 6

THE STRONG ONE

In 2019, I attended a retreat called Hearts of Beauty in Texas.

At that point in my life, I had carried the title of "the strong one" for so long, it had practically become my identity. Strong for my brother. Strong for my dad. Strong in front of others. And strong when I was falling apart inside.

But Hearts of Beauty was different. It was sacred. Safe. For the first time in a long time, I did not feel the pressure to perform or protect—I could just be. And in that space, I realized how much of my strength had come at the cost of my softness. I had built walls. I had become numb to loss. Because after losing so many people, I had developed a deeper fear: not of grief itself but of being the next one lost.

During one of the most powerful ceremonies at the retreat, we were asked to write down the things we wanted to let go of fears, pain, lies we believed about ourselves—and then release them. I remember writing down that fear of being lost, not just physically, but emotionally. Spiritually. Silently fading while trying to hold everyone else up.

And when I let that paper go, something inside me broke open. For the first time in years, I did not just feel the pain—I let it move through me. That weekend was a turning point. I realized that strength is not the absence of emotion. Real strength is letting yourself feel— and still choosing to move forward anyway.

That's when the healing really began.

As 2020 began, I felt God pressing on my heart like never before—whispering that it was time to write this book. That would help so many people heal. It did not feel small; it felt divine. I knew this was not just for me. It was bigger.

So I started fasting. Praying. Seeking God early that year, asking Him to show me what this was supposed to be.

And then… my Aunt Motice came to mind.

We had just lost my grandfather suddenly in May of 2019. Another unexpected wave of grief. But in the stillness of my prayer, God reminded me of the quiet strength she gave me years ago. Back when I was just a girl navigating the fresh loss of my mother, Aunt Motice would sit with me for hours doing puzzles. Sometimes we talked. Sometimes we did not. But it did not matter. She was there.

I picked up the phone and called her. I told her thank you for silently helping me through one of the hardest seasons of my life. For giving me space to be broken without having to explain it.

Now, years later, I was watching my own daughter begin to understand grief. And let me tell you watching your child grieve is one of the hardest things in the world, especially when you have never really been taught how to grieve yourself.

So I started journaling. Researching. Trying to find resources to help her navigate this storm.

But God said, "You are the person. You are the one."

One night, I stayed up until sunrise writing what I thought would be my first novel. It was a children's book called A Letter to My 13-Year-Old Self. A love letter. A guide. A soft place for kids walking through grief.

And when I finished it, I cried. And cried.

The next day, I woke up so heavy I could barely function. The tears just kept coming. I did not even know why they were falling the way they were.

Looking back, I think my soul knew what was happening. I was finally unearthing the grief I had buried for so long. I was facing it— not just for me, but for every little girl, every motherless child, every silent "strong one" who needed to know they weren't alone.

But I was afraid.

Afraid that publishing something so vulnerable would make me look weak. Afraid that people would not understand.

Afraid that telling my truth would change how the world saw me.

But God kept whispering…

"Tell it anyway."

So I did.

Not all at once. Not with full confidence. But with obedience.

I started writing journaling, praying, surrendering every fear that tried to rise back up. Every time I doubted if I was enough. Every time I questioned whether people would accept my truth. God reminded me that this was not about acceptance. It was about assignment.

And part of that assignment was to stop carrying the label of "the strong one" like a badge of honor and start healing the girl underneath it.

For years, I thought being strong meant being silent. I thought it meant never crying in front of people. Never admitting I was overwhelmed. Never showing the cracks in my heart. But strength like that? It is not sustainable.

The cost of being "the strong one" was that nobody checked on me.

Nobody asked if I was okay.

Nobody imagined that I needed a break, or help, or grace.

Because I wore strength so well, people assumed I did not need anything else.

But deep down, I was tired.

Tired of holding space for others while my own emotions went ignored.

Tired of pouring and never being poured into.

Tired of believing that my worth was tied to what I could survive without falling apart.

So I let go.

I let go of the fear.

I let go of the silence.

I let go of the idea that vulnerability is weakness.

Because the truth is, it takes immense strength to tell your story. To speak your pain. To own your journey.

That is what this book became for me a reclamation of my voice. A sacred offering to the younger me who was never allowed to fully grieve, and to the woman I am still becoming, who now knows she doesn't have to carry it all alone.

Reflection Prompt:

- Have you ever been labeled "the strong one"? What did that role cost you emotionally, mentally, or spiritually?

- What emotions have you buried in order to keep things together for others?

- What would it look like to give yourself permission to feel, to be vulnerable, and to ask for help?

Quote:

"You don't have to set yourself on fire to keep others warm."

— Unknown

Scripture:

"Come to me, all you who are weary and burdened, and I will give you rest."

— Matthew 11:28 (NIV)

CHAPTER 7

HEALING IN REAL TIME

In 2021, I made a decision that I did not fully understand at the time I left my daughter for three months to take a job assignment. It was one of the hardest things I have ever done as a mother. But in hindsight, it was one of the most necessary seasons of my life.

That time away was more than just about work. It became an invitation to stillness, to quiet, to truly hear from God. I found myself driving often, and my truck became my sanctuary. I spent hours listening to sermons, crying, praying, and asking God to show me what was next. I did not yet understand my assignment, but I could feel that something was shifting. That after those three months, my life would not be the same.

The years leading up to that moment had broken me in more ways than one.

Between 2018 and 2019, grief revisited me like an uninvited guest who refused to leave. I lost two uncles just six months apart. I lost Keneshia, who had been pivotal in my life during the first year after my mom passed. And then, the blow that truly gutted me—my grandfather, my mom's dad, passed away the Friday before Mother's Day.

That Mother's Day was unbearable.

I sat at the foot of my mom's vault, something I had never done before. And I cried. The weight of compounded grief of what I had lost, and what I was still carrying crushed me. That was the second hardest Mother's Day I had ever experienced. The first? That came years earlier, not long after my mom passed.

On that first Mother's Day, I thought I might be okay. I walked into church, hoping the strength I had mustered would carry me through the service. But the longer I sat there, the heavier the grief became. It wrapped around my chest like a vice. I could barely breathe. Eventually, I excused myself to the bathroom. And there, I lost it.

I wept.

I collapsed beneath the weight of everything I had tried to hold in.

My dad found me. He followed me out. We sat together in the foyer for a while, but even that space felt too tight for my emotions. So, we left. Sometimes, love looks like giving each other permission to walk away when the weight is too much.

Healing, I have learned, does not happen all at once. It is slow. It is painful. It comes in waves unexpected moments in quiet trucks and crowded bathrooms, at cemetery plots and during church services.

But that time in 2021—those three months—marked the beginning of a new kind of healing. A deeper kind. A spiritual rebuilding. God was preparing me for something. And though I could not yet see the full picture, I could feel that the pieces were starting to move into place.

Reflection Prompts:

- What moments of stillness have allowed you to reconnect with yourself or your faith?
- Have you ever recognized healing only in hindsight?
- How has grief shaped the way you experience holidays or milestones?

Quote:

> *"Sometimes you don't realize the weight of what you've been carrying until you feel the peace of letting it go."*

Scripture:

"He heals the brokenhearted and binds up their wounds."

— Psalm 147:3 (NIV)

CHAPTER 7

HEALING IN REAL TIME (PART II)

In October of 2021, my best friend lost her mother. I can still remember the phone call as if it had just happened. My spirit stirred, and I knew—my assignment was screaming louder than ever.

Just two months earlier, in August, I had moved to Hattiesburg. It was not just for a fresh start, it was intentional. My new career would require me to travel often, and being in Hattiesburg meant my daughter could stay with my best friend's sister. But in hindsight, it was more than just logistics. It was divine placement.

When I answered that call, I did not hesitate. I got up and drove straight to her apartment. At that time, we lived in the same apartment complex—what are the odds? We had known each other since high school, and after years of living in different cities, God had placed us back in the same place, at the same time. And now, only three months after I moved, her world had changed forever.

Mama Gatha.

She was not just my best friend's mom, she was another motherly figure in my life. She had taken me in years ago, fed me, loved me, hosted my baby shower, and always made sure I felt seen. We often talked about the grief of losing our moms. We laughed, we cried, and we connected over the shared experience of loss.

I can still hear her voice in Walmart. That is where we often ran into each other. Those Walmart chats were special—real, unfiltered, and full of wisdom. I did not know how much I would miss them until they were gone.

She never missed a holiday. Since 2009, she made sure I was fed—literally and emotionally. Two sweet potato pies. A saved plate of potato salad. She made it feel like home. My daughter called her "Grandma," and this loss… it cut deep. Familiar. Heavy.

But this time, I knew why I was there.

God allowed me to be there for my friend in the very way I had once needed someone to be there for me. He took all the years of my grief, all the quiet moments in trucks and at gravesides, and used them to prepare me for this moment. My pain had purpose. And it was not just for me.

I became her anchor—not because I had all the answers, but because I understood the silence. The ache. The confusion. And I did not need to fix it. I just needed to show up.

That is the beauty of healing in real time. It is messy and incomplete, but it's also sacred. It is not just about becoming whole it is about holding space for others while they're breaking, too.

Reflection Prompts:

- Has your pain ever prepared you to walk with someone else through theirs?
- What does it mean to be present without needing to fix?
- Who in your life has shown up for you during loss—and who have you shown up for?

Quote:

*"God doesn't waste pain. What
broke you will bless someone else."*

Scripture:

*"Praise be to the God... who comforts us in all our troubles, so that
we can comfort those in any trouble with the comfort we ourselves
receive from God."*

— 2 Corinthians 1:3-4 (NIV)

CHAPTER 8

THINGS I MISS MOST

G rief does not always shout. Sometimes, it whispers.
It shows up in the quietest places—folded into a song she used to hum, the smell of a favorite meal, or the moment I instinctively reach for the phone before remembering there's no one on the other end.

I miss her in a thousand little ways I never thought I would. Not just on the big days, but in the everyday moments that feel less whole without her.

I miss her laugh—the way it filled up a room and wrapped you in comfort. It had this contagious joy to it, the kind that made you forget your worries, even just for a moment.

I miss her smell. That familiar mix of her favorite lotion and the scent of home. Sometimes I catch it in a passing breeze or in the aisle of a store, and I pause… wondering if grief has found another way to remind me, she is still with me.

I miss her voice—especially when life gets hard. I still crave the way she would say, "It's going to be okay, baby," and somehow, I would believe it just because it came from her. I miss her advice. Her honesty. Her steady presence.

I miss watching her cook. No one could make a meal like she could. It was not just about the food it was the love she stirred into every dish. Holidays are not the same without her in the kitchen, humming, commanding space, making sure everyone was fed and full of love.

I miss her on my hardest days and my happiest ones. When I achieved something big graduations, motherhood, even healing I wanted her to see it. To tell me she was proud. I know she is, but I still wish I could hear her say it aloud.

I miss the way she loved. Unconditionally. Fiercely. Softly. She saw me in ways I did not even see myself. And in losing her, I have learned to see her in everything I do, because her love shaped me.

There is a certain loneliness that comes with missing someone so deeply. But there is also a certain kind of strength. Because every tear, every memory, every ache—that is love that doesn't know where to go.

So I give it back. I give it to my daughter, to my family, and to my community. I carry her legacy forward. And in doing that, I realize that what I miss most is not lost—it's planted. Deep within me.

And it blooms, in love.

Reflection Prompts:

- What are the little things you miss most about your loved one?
- How do those memories show up in your daily life?
- In what ways have you carried their love forward?

Quote:

"Grief is just love with no place to go."

— Jamie Anderson

Scripture:

"The Lord is close to the brokenhearted and saves those who are crushed in spirit."

— Psalm 34:18 (NIV)

CHAPTER 9

MOTHERHOOD

Let's talk about motherhood.

When I became a mom in 2013, the one thing I knew for certain was that I wanted to show up for my daughter in all the ways my mother could not show up for me. I did not have a complete map or model for what that would look like—but I had a vow.

A promise.

To be present. To be intentional. To be there.

2013 was one of the hardest years of my life, but even through all of it, I made a decision: I would show up for her in every way I could. I would be her safe place, her protector, her teacher, her biggest cheerleader. And I have tried—imperfectly, but wholeheartedly—to do exactly that.

Now, here I am in 2024, and she is eleven. Eleven years of motherhood. Eleven years of learning, stretching, praying, crying, healing.

And if I am honest, I feel like God is chastising me in this season. Not out of anger, but out of love. He has given me an assignment. He has placed something deep within me to birth not just in the natural, but in the spiritual. And I have been dragging my feet. He has told me to move, and I have stalled. He has opened doors, and I have hesitated.

So now He has my full attention.

Because everything around me started to fall apart. Everywhere I turned, I was getting knocked around—mentally, emotionally, financially, spiritually. I had nowhere else to go but back to Him. Back to the feet of the Father. Back to the only One who truly knows what I carry—and why.

And even now, through every test, through every delay, my daughter continues to be one of the greatest reminders of God's faithfulness in my life. She is light. She is the reason. She is a daily reminder that grief did not end my story—it gave birth to a new one.

And I will keep showing up.

Because I promised.

Becoming a mom was a pivotal turning point in my life.

Before Averi, I had been an aunt for many years. I loved my nieces deeply as if they were my own. I still remember my niece Erica standing in the foyer at my mom's funeral. She was just two years old, and even then, there was something grounding about her presence. My younger brother had three little girls, and I poured into them as much as I could. But truthfully, I thought I would always be the rich auntie. I never imagined myself becoming a mother.

But Averi changed that.

Her birth marked the beginning of my healing journey. I knew I had to heal. I had to break generational cycles. I had to be the one to stop grief from taking more than it already had. I did not want to pass on the hurt I was still carrying. I wanted her to feel safe, seen, and supported. I wanted her to know that it was okay to not be okay, something I did not always feel like I was allowed to be.

So motherhood, for me, became a mission. A mission to make memories. To capture everything with pictures and videos. To celebrate every holiday with joy and intention. To turn regular nights into pizza-making adventures. To choose presence over perfection.

I do not have as many childhood memories as I wish I did. Grief has a way of blocking out the past. But I do remember that my mom was about family. She packed the car full of cousins, and her arm was our seatbelt. She made us feel loved, even in chaos. She taught me independence, and I made sure to sow that into my daughter too.

Being a single mother taught me that our family is me and her. And I show up for her in every season. In my best and worst moments. In our shared storms. She has been my strength more times than I can count.

In 2013, when I lost Aunt Margie, it was Averi who held me together. I do not think I could have made it through without her. I call her my 2013 blessing, because that is what she is. The enemy tried to stop her from arriving because she was sent to push me into my purpose.

She carries the light of my mother. The presence. The warmth. The push.

My mom taught me to be strong, but motherhood taught me to be vulnerable too. It showed me that my grief story did not end with pain. It started peeling back layers I had not touched in years.

I remember sitting with one of my aunts and having a vision where I was my daughter's age again eleven talking to my mom. At that moment, I had been struggling with my health, and God reminded me of something I had tried to suppress: my fear of being lost. Not just physically, but emotionally. Spiritually. Worn out from carrying everyone else.

And God said, "If you're lost, who will be there for her?"

It shook me. Because no one could be my mom except my mom. And no one can be Averi's mom but me.

That moment was a wake-up call. It was time to choose healing. Time to stop suppressing grief and start confronting it. Because this story is not just for me. It is for every woman, every daughter, every motherless child trying to find her way.

Grief has purpose. Even when it does not make sense. Even when it hurts.

And I am learning that sometimes the only way through it is to tell the truth about what it took from you and what it gave you in return.

CHAPTER 10

MY FAVORITE MOVIE

My favorite movie is "Stepmom."

It is not because it's easy to watch or because it makes me laugh it is because it makes me feel. Every time I watch it, I feel every emotion: joy, heartbreak, the tension, the grace. It's one of those stories that wraps itself around your soul and gently reminds you of everything you've gained, everything you've lost, and everything you're still becoming.

The movie follows two women—one a biological mother battling terminal illness, the other a stepmom trying to navigate unfamiliar, emotional terrain. And in between them are the children. Caught in the middle but loved fiercely from both sides.

What "Stepmom" does so beautifully is show that love does not have to be perfect to be powerful. That letting go can be an act of love. That showing up, even when you are scared, even when you are unsure, matters more than anyone realizes.

Every time I watch Susan Sarandon's character prepare her children for a future she won't be a part of, I cry. Because I know that ache. I have felt the weight of absence. I have sat with the what-ifs and the never-agains. And every time Julia Roberts tries to be enough tries to be strong, tries to find her place—I feel that too.

Watching " Stepmom" reminds me of my own journey.

Of my mother, who left this earth far too soon.

Of the women who stepped in when she couldn't.

Of me trying to mother my own daughter while healing my inner child.

The movie taught me that grief and love coexist. That one does not cancel out the other. And that sometimes, the strongest love is the one that quietly says, "I may not have forever, but I'll love you for as long as I can."

That line gets me every time.

Because that's the kind of mother I want to be. The kind who loves without conditions. Who prepares her child not just for the now, but for the "what ifs." Who isn't afraid to tell the truth even when it's hard.

And that's why "Stepmom" means so much to me. It is not just a movie. It is a mirror. A reminder. A release.

It holds space for every daughter who has had to say goodbye too soon.

For every woman who has tried to fill impossible shoes.

For every mother who shows up, even when she is falling apart.

It is my favorite movie because it reminds me that even in the saddest goodbyes, there is beauty. There is love. There is legacy.

Reflection Prompts:

- What stories or movies speak to your soul and why?
- How has grief shaped the way you view love and legacy?
- In what ways are you showing up for those you love, even when it's hard?

Quote:

> *"Grief and love are conjoined; you don't get one without the other."*

— Jandy Nelson

Scripture:

> *"Now these three remains: faith, hope and love. But the greatest of these is love."*

— 1 Corinthians 13:13 (NIV)

CHAPTER 11

DIVINE SETUP

A few months ago, I had a spiritual encounter I will never forget. I was standing in a room, unsure of what I needed but desperate for something—confirmation, healing, maybe just peace. And then Apostle Beard looked at me and said:

> *"God told me to tell you... the thing that hurt you in your past is going to set you up for your purpose in this season and the next season. You will not grieve that thing anymore."*

It felt like heaven paused for a moment.

That word struck something deep in me. Because I knew exactly what "that thing" was. I had carried it quietly for years. It had shaped me, scared me, silenced me at times. It had made me question my worth, my strength, my ability to keep going.

But in that moment, I realized something was shifting.

This was not just a word of encouragement. It was a "Release."

God was saying: "I saw it all. I saw what broke you. I saw what you could not say aloud. And now I am going to use it."

The grief that once weighed me down was no longer going to define me. Instead, it would *fuel* me. It would shape my purpose, not my pain. And it would not follow me into the next season of my life.

That is the kind of God I serve—a God who doesn't waste pain. A God who repurposes heartbreak into healing. Who takes what was meant to bury you and builds something beautiful from it instead.

I walked away from that moment not just encouraged—but transformed.

Sometimes healing comes slowly. And sometimes, it shows up in a single sentence that wraps around your spirit and reminds you: You are still chosen. You are still called. You are still worthy. And your story is still unfolding.

What once hurt me no longer haunts me. I may remember it— but I do not grieve it.

Because now I know it was all part of the setup.

Reflection Prompts:

- What painful experiences in your past could God be repurposing for your future?

- Have you ever received a word that confirmed something your heart already knew?

- What would it look like to stop grieving the pain and start walking in the purpose?

Quote:

"Your pain is not wasted. God is using every broken piece to build something beautiful."

Scripture:

"And we know that in all things God works for the good of those who love him, who have been called according to his purpose."

— Romans 8:28 (NIV)

CHAPTER 12

BECOMING HER

There was a time I did not recognize myself.

I was surviving. Functioning. Smiling. But deep down, I was stuck in the pain of everything I had lost. I carried grief like a shadow—always behind me, always whispering. And yet, something inside me refused to stay broken.

Every storm, every loss, every tear was shaping me—gently, painfully, faithfully.

And now... I am becoming her.

The woman who does not apologize for healing.

The woman who knows her worth is not tied to how much she can carry.

The woman who speaks truth even when her voice shakes.

The woman her younger self dreamed of becoming.

I have learned that becoming her isn't about being perfect. It is about being "whole". It is about returning to the pieces of myself I once silenced and saying, "You belong too." It's honoring the version of me who had to smile through funerals, parent while grieving, push through fear, and still show up.

Becoming her meant choosing healing repeatedly.

It meant setting boundaries and letting go of roles that no longer served me. It meant reintroducing myself to peace, to joy, to rest. It meant realizing that I do not have to be the strong one all the time I just have to be "real."

Now, I walk with a different posture.

Not because life got easier but because I have gotten clearer. I understand who I am. Whose I am. And what I am called to do. I am not just writing this book I am living this testimony.

Becoming her means I embrace every part of my story especially the parts I once tried to hide.

Because they made me.
Because they freed me.
Because they built her.
And she is still becoming.

Reflection Prompts:

- What parts of yourself have you reclaimed in your healing journey?

- Who is the woman you're becoming—and how is she different from who you used to be?

- What would it look like to fully embrace your becoming?

Quote:

"She remembered who she was, and the game changed."

— Lalah Delia

Scripture:

"She is clothed with strength and dignity; she can laugh at the days to come."

— Proverbs 31:25 (NIV)

CHAPTER 13

THE GIRL I USED TO BE

I have been thinking a lot about the girl I used to be.

The one who sat in a hospital room, staring at machines, didn't understand. The one who held her baby brother through the night while quietly breaking inside. The one who smiled for pictures, laughed with friends, showed up for everyone and never once admitted how heavy it all was.

She was strong. So much stronger than she knew.

But she was also tired. Confused. Angry. Afraid.

She did not have the words back then to describe what she was carrying. So, she carried it all in silence trying not to inconvenience anyone with her grief, trying to be okay so that others could be too.

I think about her often. And now, instead of being ashamed of how she handled things, I hold her close.

Because she did the best she could.

She kept going when it felt impossible. She loved people through her pain. She showed up, even when no one showed up for her. And most of all, she never gave up.

I have done a lot of work to get back to her. Not to become her again but to rescue the parts of her that were buried under trauma and expectation. To tell her: "You were never too much. You were never not enough."

She needed someone to choose her. So now, I choose her.

I choose to rest over performance. Truth over silence. Wholeness over perfection.

I choose softness because that strength she wore was heavy, and she deserves to lay it down now.

And I choose to speak her name in love. Not in regret.

Because the girl I used to be? She is the reason I'm the woman I am today. And every time I look at my daughter, I see the redemption of her story unfolding.

I am not trying to erase her. I am learning to embrace her.

Because she did not just survive.

She laid the foundation for everything I have become.

Reflection Prompts:

- What would you say to your younger self today?
- What parts of her strength are you still carrying?
- What parts of her pain have you now released?

Quote:

> *"Dear younger me, you didn't deserve what happened to you but you handled it with courage far beyond your years."*

Scripture:

> *"When I was a child, I talked like a child, I thought like a child, I reasoned like a child. When I became a man, I put the ways of childhood behind me."*

> **— 1 Corinthians 13:11 (NIV)**

CHAPTER 14

A LEGACY OF LOVE

My mom's light shined really, bright.

Years later, students she once taught still come up to me to share how much of an impact she made on their lives. She was one of those people who wore many hats and walked in many callings—with grace, humor, and boldness. I still hear stories from my uncle about how she showed up for others, and I reflect often on how she cared for my dad's children from a previous marriage as if they were her own. She was a mother in every sense of the word.

I think that is why I have always connected so deeply with the movie "Stepmom." Both women in that film reminded me of my mother. She was a biological mother and a stepmother, yet her love never had limits. She embodied both strength and softness. Her presence changed people.

One of her former students once told me a story I will never forget. They had won a basketball game the night before, and the class was talking about all kinds of trash the next day. My mom let them brag, but then she stood up and said, "Alright, suit up and meet me at recess. Let's see if you can beat me." And she did. She schooled them in basketball. That was so her brave, bold, and always willing to surprise people with her resilience.

Even when she got sick, she wanted to protect us. She did not tell us she had cancer, she said there was a lump and that she needed treatment. But I was eleven, and I had already lost an aunt to cancer. When I overheard a voicemail referring to her as a "breast cancer patient," I realized she had kept the truth from us. I know it came from a place of protection, but it also taught me something important.

As I build my own legacy with my daughter, I chose "transparency."

I tell her the truth. I talk to her about life and grief and what to expect from the world because if I don't, the world will. And I would rather she hear it from me, raw and real, than be blindsided by it somewhere else.

My legacy is built on truth, strength, resilience, and tenacity.

If you ask anyone to describe me in one word, that's the one "tenacity." I showed up. I got the job done. I push through adversity. And now, I am instilling those same qualities in my daughter. Some may see it as attitude—but I know it is strength. It is fire. It is faith in action.

In 2021, God gave me a new opportunity: to homeschool my daughter, work from home, and experience life in ways I never imagined. We have created our own traditions, gone on adventures, and began shaping a life that feels rooted in joy and authenticity.

Our legacy is still unfolding—but I know this: it is being written with intention. It is built on love, truth, and purpose. And even in the places of peace I have found in the last four years, I'm still becoming. I am still building.

Because a legacy is not just what you leave behind, it's what you live out every single day.

Reflection Prompts:

- What values or truths do you want your children to carry?
- In what ways are you rewriting your family's legacy?
- How can you honor the light of those you have lost while building something new?

Quote:

"Legacy is not leaving something for people. It's leaving something in people."

— Peter Strople

Scripture:

"Her children arise and call her blessed; her husband also, and he praises her."

— Proverbs 31:28 (NIV)

CHAPTER 15

I'M STILL BECOMING

I used to think healing had a finish line.

That if I prayed hard enough, cried long enough, wrote deep enough I would arrive at "healed." I thought I would wake up one day without the weight, without the questions, without the ache.

But the truth is… I am still becoming.

And that is not a failure. That is a gift.

I am still becoming the woman God envisioned when He created me. Still growing into the voice that trembled but never went silent. Still learning how to carry joy and grief in the same breath. Still unlearning survival mode and choosing wholeness.

I no longer need to be the strongest in the room.

Now, I just want to be the most honest. The most grounded. The most present.

This journey has taught me that grief does not go away. It transforms. And so do we. I have seen myself evolve through pain, through parenting, through purpose. And though I have shed many versions of who I once was, I've never been more certain of who I'm becoming.

She is softer. But she is not weak.

She is wiser. But still curious.

She is free. Not because life got easy but because she learned to let go.

I still have moments. I still have memories that make my throat tighten. But I also have miracles. I have a daughter who makes every hard day worth it. I have a village. I have a voice. I have a story that is no longer bound by shame.

I'm still becoming.

And I'm okay with that.

Because every step, every scar, every sacred moment has led me here—to truth, to peace, to purpose. And I know now: the storm did not break me. It refined me.

I am not done. I am just beginning.

As I still become, I want to say clearly: it is okay to have a therapist.

I am grateful for mine. He walked with me through the healing process and helped me unpeel layers I did not even know were there. He taught me how to write letters to my mom and how to find a voice for the words I had been too heartbroken to say. For so long, I did not know how to communicate with someone who was no longer physically present. I wanted a sign, a dream, a visit, anything to tell me my mom was still with me.

But then, my daughter showed me something profound.

She never met my mom, not in person but she talks to her often. I woke up in the middle of the night and heard her telling her grandma about her day. Having full conversations with a woman she only knows through stories, pictures, and my prayers.

And that means everything to me.

Because it tells me I have done my part. I have kept her memory alive. I have passed down the love. My daughter may not know her grandma's face, but she knows her presence.

And that is the most powerful kind of legacy—one that speaks even when you're not in the room.

Reflection Prompts:

- What does 'becoming' look like for you in this season?
- How have your children or loved ones helped you heal?
- What part of your story do you still need to speak aloud or release?

Quote:

"Grief taught me that healing is not a destination. It's a becoming."

— Unknown

Scripture:

"I am confident of this: I will see the goodness of the Lord in the land of the living."

— Psalm 27:13 (NIV)

CHAPTER 16

MY FATHER, MY ANCHOR

There are moments when I still see the quiet strength in your eyes, Daddy the same look that told me, "We're going to be okay," even when life had left us both shattered. You were grieving too, yet you still found the courage to stand tall for us. You did the best you could with the pieces you had, and for that, I am endlessly thankful.

You carried the weight of two hearts — loving us as both Mom and Dad when the world went silent. You showed up when others didn't, and even when you didn't have the words, your presence spoke volumes. You protected me fiercely, sometimes more than I understood, but now I see it was love in its purest form of love trying to shield what was left.

I thank God for the strength He gave you in those moments. The storms we faced could have broken you, but instead, they built you into a man of quiet endurance and faith. You taught me what steadfast love looks like not through perfection, but through perseverance.

Even now, I carry your lessons with me: to keep standing, to keep believing, and to never lose hope. You taught me that being strong doesn't mean you don't feel pain — it means you don't let it stop you from showing up for the ones you love.

Thank you, Daddy, for being my anchor in the storm.

A Reflection of Gratitude

As I look back now, I see how God's hand was on both of us. He knew what we needed a father who would stand firm even when his heart was breaking. You may not have realized it then, but your quiet strength reflected His grace. Through you, I learned that love could lead even when life feels uncertain, and faith can carry us when our own strength runs out.

Your love built a foundation that still holds me today. It wasn't about doing everything perfectly; it was about never giving up. And that, Daddy, is what makes you my hero.

I thank God for choosing you to be my father for every lesson, every prayer, every protective glance that said more than words ever could.

A Prayer for My Father

Heavenly Father,

Thank You for the gift of my dad for his strength, his love, and his willingness to show up even when life was hard. Thank You for the way You held him together when grief could have undone him, and for how You used his heart to shape mine.

Bless him, Lord, for every sacrifice unseen, every tear unshed, and every moment he stood in the gap for our family. May his days be filled with peace, his heart with joy, and his spirit with the quiet knowing that his love left a legacy that will never fade.

Help me to honor him not just in words, but in the way I live, love, and keep the faith.

In Jesus' name, Amen.